Measuring
with Mr. Wiggle™
Grade 1

By Marsha Elyn Wright

Contents

Teacher's Notes 3

Possible Solutions 7

Photocopy Master for Mr. Wiggle™ 8

Photocopy Master for Mr. Wiggle™ Ruler 9

Activities 1–6:
Comparing and Measuring Lengths 10

Activities 7–12:
Comparing and Measuring Weights 16

Activities 13–19:
Measuring Perimeter 22

Investigations 1–4:
Measuring Length and Perimeter in the Real World 29

Published by Ideal School Supply
An imprint of

McGraw Hill Children's Publishing

Author: Marsha Elyn Wright
Editor: Stephanie Oberc

McGraw Hill Children's Publishing

Published by Ideal School Supply
An imprint of McGraw-Hill Children's Publishing
Copyright © 2003 McGraw-Hill Children's Publishing

All Rights Reserved • Printed in the United States of America

Limited Reproduction Permission: Permission to duplicate these materials is limited to the person for whom they are purchased. Reproduction for an entire school or school district is unlawful and strictly prohibited.

Send all inquiries to:
McGraw-Hill Children's Publishing
3195 Wilson Drive NW
Grand Rapids, Michigan 49544

Measuring with Mr. Wiggle™—grade 1
ISBN: 1-56451-994-5

1 2 3 4 5 6 7 8 9 PHXBK 08 07 06 05 04 03

The *McGraw·Hill* Companies

Teacher's Notes

This book is one in a series of books designed to develop children's mathematical thinking. Each book supports the use of Mr. Wiggle™ Counters in activities that teach key mathematical concepts.

Mr. Wiggle™ Counters are available in six different colors (red, blue, yellow, green, purple, and orange) from Ideal School Supply or your local Ideal School Supply dealer.

In *Measuring with Mr. Wiggle™*, grade 1, children use the counters to:

- understand and use vocabulary related to measurement.
- recognize the attributes of length, weight, and perimeter.
- estimate measurements.
- compare lengths and weights using words like *longer/shorter, longest/shortest,* and *heavier/lighter.*
- measure length, weight, and perimeter using nonstandard units.
- compare and order objects to find relationships.
- develop referents for units of measure.

The informal measurement activities in this book are designed to teach the concepts of measurement and develop the process skills involved in measuring. The activities support current mathematical standards.

As children engage in these measurement activities, they will make visual comparisons using concrete objects. They will use the counters to measure and will connect the repeated physical action of measuring to the repeated unit of measure. They will develop an understanding of the concepts of length, weight, and perimeter. The act of measuring commonly used objects helps connect the activities to a child's real world.

Many activities involve estimation. Estimating, or guessing, is as an important a skill in measurement as it is in all mathematics. Children develop benchmarks for units of measure through repeated experiences with estimating and measuring.

Contents

This book contains 19 activities divided into sections on length, weight, and perimeter. Each section contains similar activities, giving children the opportunity to practice and refine their skills. Possible solutions are provided on page 7.

The book also includes four investigations involving measuring objects in the real world. These investigations allow children to apply what they have learned about measurement to the world around them.

Math Skills and Understandings	Related Activities
Understand and use vocabulary related to measurement	Activities 1-19; Investigations 1-4
Estimate measurements	Activities 1-19; Investigations 1-4
Recognize the attribute of length	Activities 1-6; Investigations 1-2
Recognize the attribute of weight	Activities 7-12
Recognize the attribute of perimeter	Activities 13-19; Investigations 3-4
Measure with nonstandard units	Activities 1-19; Investigations 1-4
Make and use measurements in natural situations	Activities 1-19; Investigations 1-4
Compare objects to find relationships	Activities 7-12
Develop referents for units through estimation	Activities 1-19; Investigations 1-4
Use iteration to find length	Activities 1-6; Investigations 1-4

Suggestions for Classroom Use

The activities are sequenced by level of difficulty within each section and from section to section. Modify a section if you find it is too challenging for your children, or not challenging enough.

The activities can be introduced to the whole class using an overhead projector, the chalkboard, or sitting in a circle on the floor. Once children understand the directions for the activities, they can work in pairs, small groups, or individually at a learning center.

Encourage children to share their thinking with the whole class. Talking about their thinking and discoveries helps them clarify their thoughts and allows others to hear how they might solve the same problem a different way. Talking about how they solve problems helps children make mathematical connections and deepens their understanding. Class discussions encourage the type of thinking required for reasoning and problem solving.

Materials

You may wish to make an overhead transparency of the first activity page in each section as an introduction to the activities that follow.

For each child, pair of children, or group, you will need:
- pencils
- crayons or colored markers to match the colors of the counters
- a tub of Mr. Wiggle™ Counters in six colors: red, blue, yellow, green, purple, orange
- an activity sheet for each child or pair of children

*Note that Activities 7-12 require a balance scale.

If children are not able to record by writing numbers, make copies of page 8. The children can color each set of six Mr. Wiggle™ pictures, cut them out, and paste or glue them in place to record.

Introducing the Activities

Before beginning instruction, it is important to allow time for children to freely explore the Mr. Wiggle™ Counters. This will allow them to satisfy their curiosity about the counters before they use them as measuring tools. Encourage children to compare the counters and tell how they are alike and how they are different. Ask them to name the different colors.

When you introduce a section of the book, lead children through the first activity in that section. Discuss the directions and how to record their work. Encourage children to guess (estimate) before measuring. Point out that a guess does not have to be correct. Also, due to the nature of the Mr. Wiggle™ Counters, measurements will not be exact. For example, *about five counters long* is an acceptable measurement. You may want to model that language as you introduce the activities. When reviewing an activity as a group, encourage children to talk about their discoveries. This will help them make connections and clarify their thinking.

Mathematical Content by Section

Activities 1-6: Measuring length using nonstandard units. Children develop a sense of length as they compare lengths to determine *longer/shorter* and *longest/shortest* objects. They make estimates and then use Mr. Wiggle™ Counters to measure objects and animals as well as common objects.

Activities 7-12: Measuring weight using nonstandard units. Children develop a sense of weight as they compare weights to determine *heavier/lighter* and *heaviest/lightest* objects. They use a balance to compare different groups of Mr. Wiggle™ Counters. They develop an understanding of the terms *heavier* and *lighter* and learn that when both sides balance the weights are *the same*. They use that knowledge to estimate and then measure how many Mr. Wiggle™ Counters will balance common classroom objects.

Activities 13-19: Measuring perimeter using nonstandard units. Children develop a sense of perimeter as they estimate and then use Mr. Wiggle™ counters to measure the distances around the outsides of common shapes.

Investigations 1-4: Measuring length and perimeter using nonstandard units. Children use Mr. Wiggle™ Counters to explore the physical attributes of common objects by measuring their length and perimeter. They make use of a Mr. Wiggle™ ruler to measure objects.

Possible Solutions

These are possible solutions.

Activity

1 A   Vine 1 is about 4 counters long.
      Vine 2 is about 6 counters long.
      Vine 2 is longer.
1 B   Vine 3 is about 5 counters long.
      Vine 4 is about 3 counters long.
      Vine 4 is shorter.

2   Leaf 1 is about 2 counters long.
      Leaf 2 is about 3 counters long.
      Leaf 3 is about 1 counter long.
      Leaf 2 is longest.
      Leaf 3 is shortest.

3 A   About 2 counters
3 B   About 4 counters

4   Answers will vary.

5   Answers will vary.

6   Answers will vary.

7 A   The stone is heavier.
7 B   The counter is lighter.

8 A   Heavier group: 6 counters
8 B   Lighter group: 5 counters

9 A   Lighter group: 4 counters
9 B   Heavier group: 6 counters

10   Answers will vary.

11   Answers will vary.

12   Answers will vary.
13 A About 10 counters
13 B About 8 counters
13 C Fence A

14 A About 40 counters
14 B About 13 counters

15 A About 10 counters
15 B Answers will vary.

Activity

16 A About 20 counters
16 B About 15 medium counters

17 A About 25 counters
17 B About 11 counters

18   About 20 counters

19 A About 6 counters
19 B About 6 counters

Investigation

1 A   (The ruler is about six inches long.)
      Objects about five inches long such as a marker.
1 B   Objects about four inches long such as a crayon.
1 C   Objects about three inches long such as a glue stick.

Investigation

2 A   Objects about 6 inches long such as a stapler.
2 B   Objects about 3 inches long such as an eraser.

Investigation 3 Answers will vary.

Investigation 4 Answers will vary.

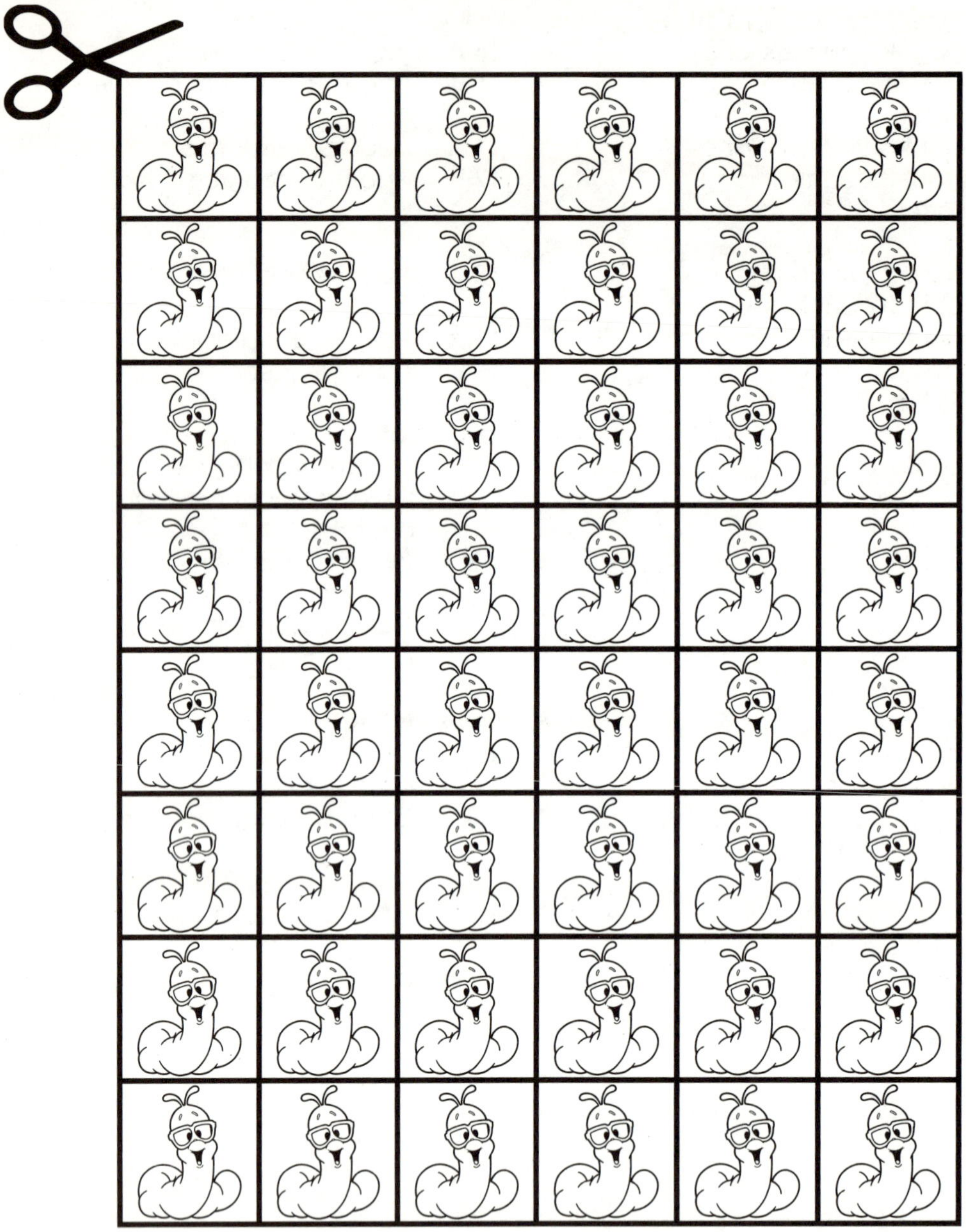

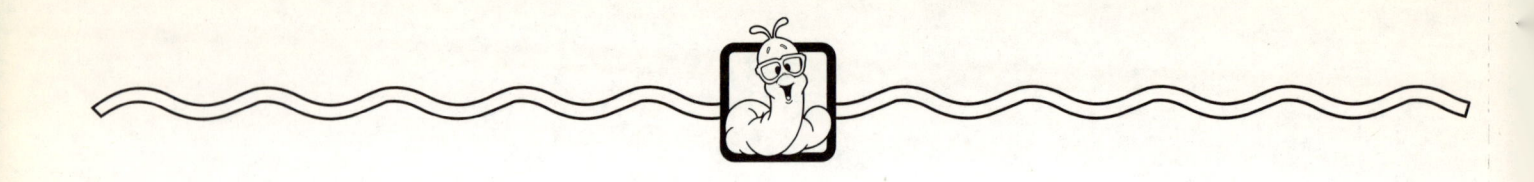

Make a Mr. Wiggle™ ruler

Name_____

Use crayons or colored markers, scissors, and glue.

Make a ruler.

Color the pictures of Mr. Wiggle.
Cut them out.
Glue the pictures on the ruler shape.
Cut out the ruler.

Compare, estimate, and measure length

Name_____

Activity 1

Use Mr. Wiggle™ Counters.
Record your work.

A. Which vine is **longer**? Circle it.
Guess the length. Use counters to measure.

           Guess   Measure

Vine 1 _____   _____

Vine 2 _____   _____

1

2

B. Which vine is **shorter**? Circle it.
Guess the length. Use counters to measure.

           Guess   Measure

Vine 3 _____   _____

Vine 4 _____   _____

3

4

© McGraw-Hill Children's Publishing   1-56451-994-5 *Measuring with Mr. Wiggle*™

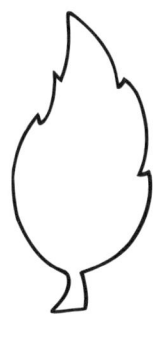

Compare, estimate, and measure length

Name_____

Activity 2

Use Mr. Wiggle™ Counters.
Record your work.

Which leaf is **longest**? Circle it.
Which leaf is **shortest**? Draw an **X** over it.
Guess the length. Use counters to measure.

	Guess	Measure
Leaf 1	_____	_____
Leaf 2	_____	_____
Leaf 3	_____	_____

1   **2**   **3**

© McGraw-Hill Children's Publishing

1-56451-994-5 *Measuring with Mr. Wiggle*™

Estimate and measure length

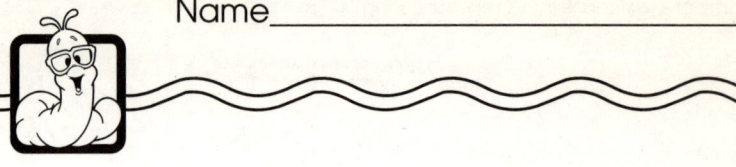

Name_____

Activity 3

Use Mr. Wiggle™ Counters and medium paper counters. Record your work.

A. How long is the bug?
Guess. Use counters to measure.

Guess _____

Measure _____

B. How long is the bug?
Guess. Use counters to measure.

Guess _____

Measure _____

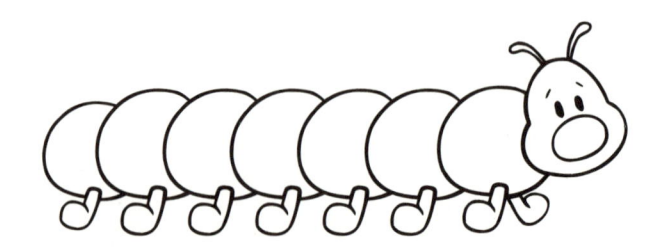

© McGraw-Hill Children's Publishing

1-56451-994-5 *Measuring with Mr. Wiggle*™

Estimate and measure length

Name _____

Activity 4

Use Mr. Wiggle™ Counters. Record your work.

A. How long is your pencil ?

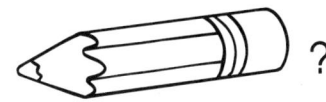

Guess. Use counters to measure.

Guess _____   Measure _____

B. How long is your ruler ?

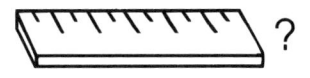

Guess. Use counters to measure.

Guess _____   Measure _____

C. How long are your scissors ?

Guess. Use counters to measure.

Guess _____   Measure _____

D. How long is your eraser ?

Guess. Use counters to measure.

Guess _____   Measure _____

© McGraw-Hill Children's Publishing   1-56451-994-5 *Measuring with Mr. Wiggle*™

Estimate and measure length

Name_____

Activity 5

Use Mr. Wiggle™ Counters. Record your work.

Trace your foot.

A. How long is your foot?

Guess. Use counters to measure.

Guess _____   Measure _____

B. How long is your big toe?

Guess. Use counters to measure.

Guess _____   Measure _____

C. How wide is your foot?

Guess _____   Measure _____

Estimate and measure length

Name_____

Activity 6

Use Mr. Wiggle™ Counters.
Record your work.

A. Find a picture.
How long is the picture ?

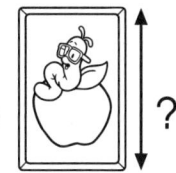

Guess. Use counters to measure.

Guess _____   Measure _____

B. How wide is the picture ?

Guess. Use counters to measure.

Guess _____   Measure _____

C. Find something about as long as the .
Use counters to measure.

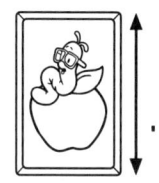

What thing did you find? _____

D. Find something about as wide as the .
Use counters to measure.

What thing did you find? _____

Compare and measure weight   Name_____

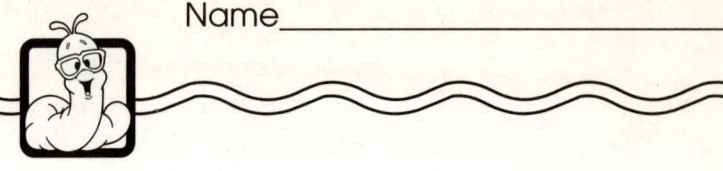

Activity 7

Use Mr. Wiggle™ Counters.

Use a ⚖. Record your work.

A. Find a small stone.
   Hold the stone in one hand. Hold a counter in the other hand.
   Circle which feels **heavier**.

   Stone   Counter

   Use the ⚖ to check.

B. Find a medium stone.
   Hold the stone in one hand. Hold a counter in the other hand.
   Circle which feels **lighter**.

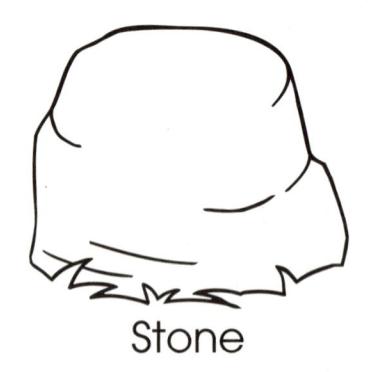

   Stone   Counter

   Use the ⚖ to check.

Compare and measure weight

Name_____

Activity 8

Use Mr. Wiggle™ Counters.

Use a ⚖. Record your work.

A. Compare the two groups.

Which group is **heavier**? Guess. Use the ⚖ to check.

Circle the **heavier** group.

B. Compare the two groups.

Which group is **lighter**? Guess. Use the ⚖ to check.

Circle the **lighter** group.

17

© McGraw-Hill Children's Publishing   1-56451-994-5 Measuring with Mr. Wiggle™

Estimate and measure weight

Name_____

Activity 9

Use Mr. Wiggle™ Counters.

Use a ⚖. Record your work.

A. Compare the two groups.

Which group is **lighter**? Guess. Use the ⚖ to check.

Circle the **lighter** group.

B. Compare the two groups.

Which group is **heavier**? Guess. Use the ⚖ to check.

Circle the **heavier** group.

Estimate and measure weight

Name_____

Activity 10

Use Mr. Wiggle™ Counters.

Use a ⚖ . Record your work.

A. How many counters weigh the same as 1 crayon?

Guess. Measure with a ⚖ and 🐛 .

Guess _____

Measure _____

B. How many counters weigh the same as 3 crayons?

Guess. Measure with a ⚖ and 🐛 .

Guess _____

Measure _____

C. How many counters weigh the same as 5 crayons?

Guess. Measure with a ⚖ and 🐛 .

Guess _____

Measure _____

Estimate and measure weight

Name_____

Activity 11

Use Mr. Wiggle™ Counters.

Use a ⚖. Record your work.

A. How many counters will balance your box of crayons?

Guess. Use counters and the ⚖ to measure.

Guess _____

Measure _____

B. Find something you think weighs the same as your box of crayons.

What thing did you find? _____

Draw a picture of it on the back of this paper.

C. Use the ⚖ to measure.

Does your new object weigh about the same as your box of crayons? _____

Estimate and measure weight

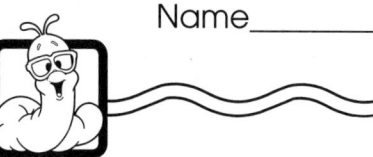

Name_____

Activity 12

Use Mr. Wiggle™ Counters.
Use a ⚖. Record your work.

A. Find things to balance.
Guess how many counters will balance each thing.
Use the ⚖ to check.

Name of Thing	Guess	Weigh

B. Find things that equal each group of counters.
Use the ⚖ to check.

Group of Counters	Name of Thing
8	
16	
20	

Estimate and measure perimeter

Activity 13

Use Mr. Wiggle™ Counters.
Record your work.

A. How many counters go around the fence?
Guess. Use counters to measure.

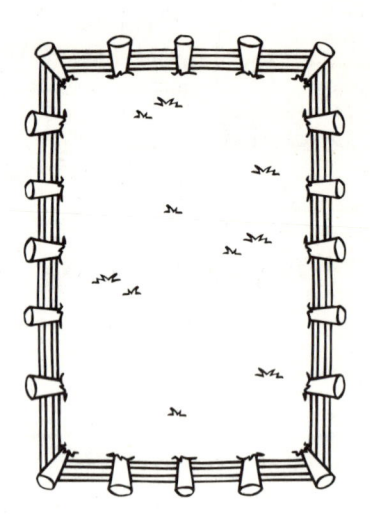

Guess _____

Measure _____

B. How many counters go around the fence?
Guess. Use counters to measure.

Guess _____

Measure _____

C. Which fence is bigger?

_____

Estimate and measure perimeter

Name_____

Activity 14

Use Mr. Wiggle™ Counters.
Record your work.

A. How many counters go around the school?
Guess. Use counters to measure.

Guess _____   Measure _____

B. How many counters go around the car?
Guess. Use counters to measure.

Guess _____   Measure _____

23

Estimate and measure perimeter

Activity 15

Use Mr. Wiggle™ Counters.
Record your work.

A. How many counters go around the book?
Guess. Use counters to measure.

Guess _____

Measure _____

B. Find a book.
How many counters go around your book?
Guess. Use counters to measure.

Guess _____

Measure _____

Estimate and measure perimeter

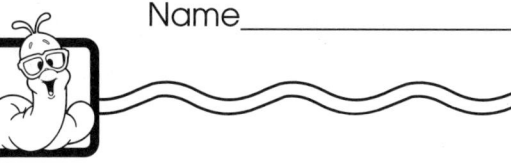

Name_____

Activity 16

Use Mr. Wiggle™ Counters. Record your work.

A. How many counters go around the fence?

Guess _____   Measure _____

B. How many counters go around the garden?

Guess _____   Measure _____

25

© McGraw-Hill Children's Publishing

1-56451-994-5 *Measuring with Mr. Wiggle*™

Estimate and measure perimeter

Name_____

Activity 17

Use Mr. Wiggle™ Counters.
Record your work.

A. How many counters go around the door?

Guess _____

Measure _____

B. How many counters go around the window?

Guess _____

Measure _____

Estimate and measure perimeter

Activity 18

Use Mr. Wiggle™ Counters.
Record your work.

A. Draw a new house for Mr. Wiggle.
Make the house 6 counters long and 4 counters high.
It will be about 20 counters around
the outside of the house.

Estimate and measure perimeter

Name_____

Activity 19

Use Mr. Wiggle™ Counters.
Record your work.

A. How many counters go
around the circle?
Guess. Use counters to measure.

Guess _____

Measure _____

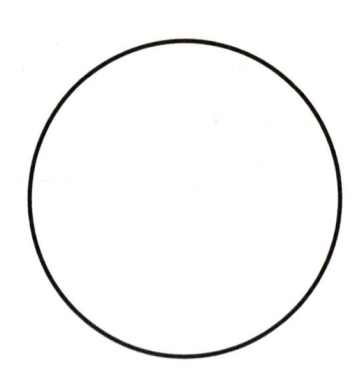

B. How many counters go
around the rectangle?
Guess. Use counters to measure.

Guess _____

Measure _____